MW00899031

Just in Case

A Workbook

Just in Case

A Workbook

A Record of Vital Information
in the Event of Emergency, Natural
Disaster, Prolonged Illness, or Death

Amy Levine

Legal Disclaimer and Copyright

This book is intended as a reference volume only, not as a legal manual. The information provided is designed to help make informed decisions about finalizing the affairs of a loved one, but is not intended as a substitute for legal advice.

© 2013 Amy Levine
Published by Vienna Woods Media

All rights reserved. No part of this publication may be reproduced or transmitted in any form or any means, electronic or mechanical, including photocopying, recording, or any other information storage and retrieval system, without written permission of the author. Brief quotations embodied in critical articles and reviews are permitted.

ISBN 13: 978-1492104100

Contents

Introduction

Emergencies, accidents, natural disasters, prolonged illness and even death can happen anytime. Don't be caught off guard – recording all relevant personal, family, financial, residential, and property information in one document, including your final wishes – will help both you and your family in times of upheaval.

In the event of a prolonged illness or death, having access to account numbers, logins and passwords can allow a family to handle affairs directly and bypass a great deal of bureaucratic red tape. Knowing where to find crucial documents, such as your medical directive, power of attorney, or last will and testament can save time for your family and spare them stress.

Use this workbook to clearly outline your final wishes as well as designate how your personal possessions should be distributed. Then give this information to your lawyer to put in your will because only a valid and binding will ensures your wishes will be upheld.

Don't assume it will all be worked out once you're gone! Many families will face disputes over whether their loved one will be cremated or buried and who gets what if it's not clearly stated in a will. Family feuds have erupted over the smallest items that hold sentimental, personal, or monetary value.

Without a doubt, recording all this information is a tedious chore. My suggestion is to devote a day to sit down and power through it. Then when it's done, it's done! You can wipe your hands of it and feel confident knowing that everything is in order – just in case.

How to Use This Book

Fill out as much information as possible. Remember: the more information you provide, the easier it will be for your family.

The workbook is also available as a writable PDF at www.LastChapterConcierge.com. If you are using the PDF, simply click on the shaded boxes and type in your information. Be sure to keep one original file and create a "Save As" file for your personal records. The PDF is designed with side-bar navigation that allows the reader to click on any chapter or sub-header and be linked directly to that page. For a drop-down menu of sub-headers in each chapter, click on the chapter title. Clicking on any entry in the Table of Contents will also link to it directly.

Personal and Family Information

You

Name _____
Phone number _____
Social Security number _____
Driver's license number, including state _____
Date of birth _____
Blood type _____
Height _____
Weight _____
Eye color _____
Hair _____
Organ donor _____
Allergies _____
Medications _____
School or work _____
    Web site _____
    Location _____
    Phone number _____
    Contact person _____
    E-mail _____

Physician

    Name _____
    Web site _____
    Location _____
    Phone number _____
    E-mail _____

Specialist

    Name _____

    Web site _____

    Location _____

    Phone number _____

    E-mail _____

Specialist

    Name _____

    Web site _____

    Location _____

    Phone number _____

    E-mail _____

Specialist

    Name _____

    Web site _____

    Location _____

    Phone number _____

    E-mail _____

Specialist

    Name _____

    Web site _____

    Location _____

    Phone number _____

    E-mail _____

Dentist

    Name _____

    Web site _____

    Location _____

    Phone number _____

    E-mail _____

Health Insurance

    Insurance provider _____

    Policy number _____

    Web site _____

    Location _____

    Phone number _____

    E-mail _____

Account number _____

User name _____

Password _____

If payment is made automatically online

    Bank _____

    Web site _____

    Phone number _____

    E-mail _____

    Account number _____

    Amount _____

    User name _____

    Password _____

Spouse

Name _____

Phone number _____

Social Security number _____

Driver's license number, including state _____

Date of birth _____

Blood type _____

Height _____

Weight _____

Eye color _____

Hair _____

Organ donor _____

Allergies _____

Medications _____

School or work _____

    Web site _____

    Location _____

    Phone number _____

    Contact person _____

    E-mail _____

Physician

Name _____

Web site _____

Location _____

Phone number _____

E-mail _____

Specialist
    Name _____
    Web site _____
    Location _____
    Phone number _____
    E-mail _____

Specialist
    Name _____
    Web site _____
    Location _____
    Phone number _____
    E-mail _____

Specialist
    Name _____
    Web site _____
    Location _____
    Phone number _____
    E-mail _____

Specialist
    Name _____
    Web site _____
    Location _____
    Phone number _____
    E-mail _____

Dentist
    Name _____
    Web site _____
    Location _____
    Phone number _____
    E-mail _____

Health Insurance
    Insurance provider _____
    Policy number _____
    Web site _____
    Location _____
    Phone number _____
    E-mail _____

Account number _____
User name _____
Password _____

If payment is made automatically online

    Bank _____
    Web site _____
    Phone number _____
    E-mail _____
    Account number _____
    Amount _____
    User name _____
    Password _____

Ex-Spouse

Name _____
Phone number _____
School or work _____

    Web site _____
    Location _____
    Phone number _____
    Contact person _____
    E-mail _____

Child #1

Name _____
Phone number _____
Social Security number _____
Driver's license number, including state _____
Date of birth _____
Blood type _____
Height _____
Weight _____
Eye color _____
Hair _____
Organ donor _____
Allergies _____
Medications _____
School or work _____

Web site _____

Location _____

Phone number _____

Contact person _____

E-mail _____

Location if living away from home

Address _____

Phone number _____

Contact person _____

Phone number _____

Physician

Name _____

Web site _____

Location _____

Phone number _____

E-mail _____

Specialist

Name _____

Web site _____

Location _____

Phone number _____

E-mail _____

Specialist

Name _____

Web site _____

Location _____

Phone number _____

E-mail _____

Specialist

Name _____

Web site _____

Location _____

Phone number _____

E-mail _____

Specialist

    Name _____

    Web site _____

    Location _____

    Phone number _____

    E-mail _____

Dentist

    Name _____

    Web site _____

    Location _____

    Phone number _____

    E-mail _____

Health Insurance

    Insurance provider _____

    Policy number _____

    Web site _____

    Location _____

    Phone number _____

    E-mail _____

    Account number _____

    User name _____

    Password _____

    If payment is made automatically online

        Bank _____

        Web site _____

        Phone number _____

        E-mail _____

        Account number _____

        Amount _____

        User name _____

        Password _____

Child #2

    Name _____

    Phone number _____

    Social Security number _____

    Driver's license number, including state _____

    Date of birth _____

Blood type _____

Height _____

Weight _____

Eye color _____

Hair _____

Organ donor _____

Allergies _____

Medications _____

School or work _____

    Web site _____

    Location _____

    Phone number _____

    Contact person _____

    E-mail _____

Location if living away from home

    Address _____

    Phone number _____

    Contact person _____

    Phone number _____

Physician

    Name _____

    Web site _____

    Location _____

    Phone number _____

    E-mail _____

Specialist

    Name _____

    Web site _____

    Location _____

    Phone number _____

    E-mail _____

Specialist

    Name _____

    Web site _____

    Location _____

    Phone number _____

    E-mail _____

Specialist

    Name _____

    Web site _____

    Location _____

    Phone number _____

    E-mail _____

Dentist

    Name _____

    Web site _____

    Location _____

    Phone number _____

    E-mail _____

Health Insurance

    Insurance provider _____

    Policy number _____

    Web site _____

    Location _____

    Phone number _____

    E-mail _____

    Account number _____

    User name _____

    Password _____

    If payment is made automatically online

        Bank _____

        Web site _____

        Phone number _____

        E-mail _____

        Account number _____

        Amount _____

        User name _____

        Password _____

Child #2

    Name _____

    Phone number _____

    Social Security number _____

    Driver's license number, including state _____

    Date of birth _____

Blood type _____

Height _____

Weight _____

Eye color _____

Hair _____

Organ donor _____

Allergies _____

Medications _____

School or work _____

    Web site _____

    Location _____

    Phone number _____

    Contact person _____

    E-mail _____

Location if living away from home

    Address _____

    Phone number _____

    Contact person _____

    Phone number _____

Physician

    Name _____

    Web site _____

    Location _____

    Phone number _____

    E-mail _____

Specialist

    Name _____

    Web site _____

    Location _____

    Phone number _____

    E-mail _____

Specialist

    Name _____

    Web site _____

    Location _____

    Phone number _____

    E-mail _____

Specialist

    Name _____

    Web site _____

    Location _____

    Phone number _____

    E-mail _____

Specialist

    Name _____

    Web site _____

    Location _____

    Phone number _____

    E-mail _____

Dentist

    Name _____

    Web site _____

    Location _____

    Phone number _____

    E-mail _____

Health Insurance

    Insurance provider _____

    Policy number _____

    Web site _____

    Location _____

    Phone number _____

    E-mail _____

    Account number _____

    User name _____

    Password _____

    If payment is made automatically online

        Bank _____

        Web site _____

        Phone number _____

        E-mail _____

        Account number _____

        Amount _____

        User name _____

        Password _____

Child #3

Name _____
Phone number _____
Social Security number _____
Driver's license number, including state _____
Date of birth _____
Blood type _____
Height _____
Weight _____
Eye color _____
Hair _____
Organ donor _____
Allergies _____
Medications _____
School or work _____
    Web site _____
    Location _____
    Phone number _____
    Contact person _____
    E-mail _____
Location if living away from home
    Address _____
    Phone number _____
    Contact person _____
    Phone number _____

Physician
Name _____
Web site _____
Location _____
Phone number _____
E-mail _____

Specialist
Name _____
Web site _____
Location _____
Phone number _____
E-mail _____

Specialist

Name _____

Web site _____

Location _____

Phone number _____

E-mail _____

Specialist

Name _____

Web site _____

Location _____

Phone number _____

E-mail _____

Specialist

Name _____

Web site _____

Location _____

Phone number _____

E-mail _____

Dentist

Name _____

Web site _____

Location _____

Phone number _____

E-mail _____

Health Insurance

Insurance provider _____

Policy number _____

Web site _____

Location _____

Phone number _____

E-mail _____

Account number _____

User name _____

Password _____

If payment is made automatically online

Bank _____

Web site _____

Phone number _____

E-mail _____

Account number _____

Amount _____

User name _____

Password _____

Sibling #1

Name _____

Phone number _____

Social Security number _____

Driver's license number, including state _____

Date of birth _____

Blood type _____

Height _____

Weight _____

Eye color _____

Hair _____

Organ donor _____

Allergies _____

Medications _____

School or work _____

    Web site _____

    Location _____

    Phone number _____

    Contact person _____

    E-mail _____

Sibling #2

Name _____

Phone number _____

Social Security number _____

Driver's license number, including state _____

Date of birth _____

Blood type _____

Height _____

Weight _____

Eye color _____

Hair _____

Organ donor _____

Allergies _____

Medications _____

School or work _____

    Web site _____

    Location _____

    Phone number _____

    Contact person _____

    E-mail _____

Sibling #3

Name _____

Phone number _____

Social Security number _____

Driver's license number, including state _____

Date of birth _____

Blood type _____

Height _____

Weight _____

Eye color _____

Hair _____

Organ donor _____

Allergies _____

Medications _____

School or work _____

    Web site _____

    Location _____

    Phone number _____

    Contact person _____

    E-mail _____

Mother

Name _____

Phone number _____

Social Security number _____

Driver's license number, including state _____

Date of birth _____

Blood type _____

Height _____

Weight _____

Eye color _____

Hair _____

Organ donor _____

Allergies _____

Medications _____

School or work _____

    Web site _____

    Location _____

    Phone number _____

    Contact person _____

    E-mail _____

Father

Name _____

Phone number _____

Social Security number _____

Driver's license number, including state _____

Date of birth _____

Blood type _____

Height _____

Weight _____

Eye color _____

Hair _____

Organ donor _____

Allergies _____

Medications _____

School or work _____

    Web site _____

    Location _____

    Phone number _____

    Contact person _____

    E-mail _____

Step-Parent

Name _____

Phone number _____

Social Security number _____

Driver's license number, including state _____

Date of birth _____

Blood type _____
Height _____
Weight _____
Eye color _____
Hair _____
Organ donor _____
Allergies _____
Medications _____
School or work _____
      Web site _____
      Location _____
      Phone number _____
      Contact person _____
      E-mail _____

Step-Parent

Name _____
Phone number _____
Social Security number _____
Driver's license number, including state _____
Date of birth _____
Blood type _____
Height _____
Weight _____
Eye color _____
Hair _____
Organ donor _____
Allergies _____
Medications _____
School or work _____
      Web site _____
      Location _____
      Phone number _____
      Contact person _____
      E-mail _____

Emergency Contacts

Emergency Contact #1

Name _____
Relation to you or your family _____
Location _____
Phone number _____
E-mail _____
School or work _____
    Web site _____
    Location _____
    Phone number _____
    Contact person _____
    E-mail _____

Emergency Contact #2

Name _____
Relation to you or your family _____
Location _____
Phone number _____
E-mail _____
School or work _____
    Web site _____
    Location _____
    Phone number _____
    Contact person _____
    E-mail _____

Emergency Contact #3

Name _____
Relation to you or your family _____
Location _____
Phone number _____
E-mail _____
School or work _____
    Web site _____
    Location _____
    Phone number _____
    Contact person _____
    E-mail _____

Emergency Contact #4

Name _____
Relation to you or your family _____
Location _____
Phone number _____
E-mail _____
School or work _____
    Web site _____
    Location _____
    Phone number _____
    Contact person _____
    E-mail _____

Pets

Pet #1

Name _____

Age _____

Type of animal _____

Breed _____

Location of medical files _____

Allergies _____

Medications _____

Veterinarian

Name _____

Web site _____

Location _____

Phone number _____

E-mail _____

Groomer

Name _____

Web site _____

Location _____

Phone number _____

E-mail _____

Trainer

Name _____

Web site _____

Location _____

Phone number _____

E-mail _____

Kennel

    Name _____

    Web site _____

    Location _____

    Phone number _____

    E-mail _____

Pet Insurance

    Insurance provider _____

    Policy number _____

    Web site _____

    Location _____

    Phone number _____

    E-mail _____

    Account number _____

Emergency contact for pet

    Name _____

    Relation to you or your family _____

    Location _____

    Phone number _____

    E-mail _____

    School or work _____

        Web site _____

        Location _____

        Phone number _____

        Contact person _____

        E-mail _____

Pet #2

    Name _____

    Age _____

    Type of animal _____

    Breed _____

    Location of medical files _____

    Allergies _____

    Medications _____

Veterinarian

Name _____
Web site _____
Location _____
Phone number _____
E-mail _____

Groomer

Name _____
Web site _____
Location _____
Phone number _____
E-mail _____

Trainer

Name _____
Web site _____
Location _____
Phone number _____
E-mail _____

Kennel

Name _____
Web site _____
Location _____
Phone number _____
E-mail _____

Pet Insurance

Insurance provider _____
Policy number _____
Web site _____
Location _____
Phone number _____
E-mail _____
Account number _____

Emergency contact for pet

Name _____
Relation to you or your family _____
Location _____
Phone number _____

E-mail _____
School or work _____
    Web site _____
    Location _____
    Phone number _____
    Contact person _____
    E-mail _____

Livestock/large animal(s)

Name _____
Age _____
Type of animal _____
Breed _____
Location of medical files _____
Allergies _____
Medication _____
Contact person/barn manager _____
Phone number _____
Location of animal _____
    Web site _____
    Location _____
    Phone number _____
    Contact person _____
    E-mail _____

Veterinarian
Name _____
Web site _____
Location _____
Phone number _____
E-mail _____

Farrier
Name _____
Web site _____
Location _____
Phone number _____
E-mail _____

Large Animal Insurance

    Insurance provider _____

    Policy number _____

    Web site _____

    Location _____

    Phone number _____

    E-mail _____

    Account number _____

Emergency contact for large animal

    Name _____

    Relation to you or your family _____

    Location _____

    Phone number _____

    E-mail _____

    School or work _____

        Web site _____

        Location _____

        Phone number _____

        Contact person _____

        E-mail _____

In case of emergency or death, who should get your animal(s)

    Name _____

    Relation to you or your family _____

    Location _____

    Phone number _____

    E-mail _____

    School or work _____

        Web site _____

        Location _____

        Phone number _____

        Contact person _____

        E-mail _____

Contacts

Attorney

Name _____
Web site _____
Location _____
Phone number _____
E-mail _____

Accountant

Name _____
Web site _____
Location _____
Phone number _____
E-mail _____

Church, Synagogue, or Spiritual Leader

Name _____
Web site _____
Location _____
Phone number _____
E-mail _____

Realtor

Name _____
Web site _____
Location _____
Phone number _____
E-mail _____

Handyman

Name _____
Web site _____
Location _____
Phone number _____
E-mail _____

Plumber

Name _____
Web site _____
Location _____
Phone number _____
E-mail _____

Electrician

Name _____
Web site _____
Location _____
Phone number _____
E-mail _____

Painter

Name _____
Web site _____
Location _____
Phone number _____
E-mail _____

Contractor

Name _____
Web site _____
Location _____
Phone number _____
E-mail _____

Gardner/landscaping/trees

Name _____
Web site _____
Location _____
Phone number _____
E-mail _____

Windows

Name _____
Web site _____
Location _____
Phone number _____
E-mail _____

Housecleaner

Name _____
Web site _____
Location _____
Phone number _____
E-mail _____

Property and Real Estate

Home or Residence

Location of the deed _____

Location of property _____

Title _____

Current value _____

When purchased _____

Owned outright? _____

Amount due on mortgage _____

County or assessor number _____

Real estate tax bill from year prior _____

If a bank holds the deed or mortgage to the property

Bank _____

Web site _____

Location _____

Phone number _____

E-mail _____

Account number _____

User name _____

Password _____

If payment is made automatically online

Bank _____

Web site _____

Phone number _____

E-mail _____

Account number _____

Amount _____

User name _____

Password _____

If a mortgage company owns the property

Mortgage company _____

Web site _____

Location _____

Phone number _____

E-mail _____

Account number _____

User name _____

Password _____

If payment is made automatically online

Bank _____

Web site _____

Phone number _____

E-mail _____

Account number _____

Amount _____

User name _____

Password _____

Home Insurance

Insurance company _____

Policy number _____

Web site _____

Location _____

Phone number _____

E-mail _____

Account number _____

User name _____

Password _____

If payment is made automatically online

Bank _____

Web site _____

Phone number _____

E-mail _____

Account number _____

Amount _____

User name _____

Password _____

Homeowners Association

    Homeowners association _____

    Web site _____

    Location _____

    Phone number _____

    E-mail _____

    Account number _____

    If payment is made automatically online

        Web site _____

        Phone number _____

        E-mail _____

        Account number _____

        Amount _____

        User name _____

        Password _____

Additional Real Estate

    Location of the deed _____

    Location of property _____

    Title _____

    Current value _____

    When purchased _____

    Owned outright? _____

    Amount due on mortgage _____

    County or assessor number _____

    Real estate tax bill from year prior _____

    If payment is made automatically online

        Bank _____

        Web site _____

        Phone number _____

        E-mail _____

        Account number _____

        Amount _____

        User name _____

        Password _____

If a bank holds the deed or mortgage to the property

        Bank _____

        Web site _____

        Location _____

Phone number _____

E-mail _____

Account number _____

User name _____

Password _____

If payment is made automatically online

Bank _____

Web site _____

Phone number _____

E-mail _____

Account number _____

Amount _____

User name _____

Password _____

If a mortgage company owns the property

Mortgage company _____

Web site _____

Location _____

Phone number _____

E-mail _____

Account number _____

User name _____

Password _____

If payment is made automatically online

Bank _____

Web site _____

Phone number _____

E-mail _____

Account number _____

Amount _____

User name _____

Password _____

Insurance

Insurance company _____

Policy number _____

Web site _____

Location _____

Phone number _____

E-mail _____

Account number _____

User name _____

Password _____

If payment is made automatically online

Bank _____

Web site _____

Phone number _____

E-mail _____

Account number _____

Amount _____

User name _____

Password _____

Leased Apartment or Residence

Residence

Name of property _____
Location _____
Web site _____
Landlord _____
Phone number _____
Location of lease _____
Location of extra keys _____
If payment is made automatically online

    Bank _____
    Web site _____
    Phone number _____
    E-mail _____
    Account number _____
    Amount _____
    User name _____
    Password _____

Renter's Insurance

Insurance company _____
Policy number _____
Web site _____
Location _____
Phone number _____
E-mail _____
Account number _____

User name _____

Password _____

If payment is made automatically online

      Bank _____

      Web site _____

      Phone number _____

      E-mail _____

      Account number _____

      Amount _____

      User name _____

      Password _____

Housecleaner

Name _____

Web site _____

Location _____

Phone number _____

E-mail _____

Vehicles

Vehicle #1

If the vehicle is owned outright

    Location of title _____

    Make and model of vehicle _____

    Color _____

    License plate number _____

    VIN _____

    Location of extra keys _____

    Current value _____

If there is a bank note for the vehicle

    Bank _____

    Web site _____

    Location _____

    Phone number _____

    E-mail _____

    Account number _____

    If payment is made automatically online

        Bank _____

        Web site _____

        Phone number _____

        E-mail _____

        Account number _____

        Amount _____

        User name _____

        Password _____

Vehicle Insurance

    Insurance company _____

    Policy number _____

    Web site _____

    Location _____

    Phone number _____

    E-mail _____

    Account number _____

    If payment is made automatically online

        Bank _____

        Web site _____

        Phone number _____

        E-mail _____

        Account number _____

        Amount _____

        User name _____

        Password _____

Vehicle #2

If the vehicle is owned outright

    Location of title _____

    Make and model of vehicle _____

    Color _____

    License plate number _____

    VIN _____

    Location of extra keys _____

    Current value _____

If there is a bank note for the vehicle

    Bank _____

    Web site _____

    Location _____

    Phone number _____

    E-mail _____

    Account number _____

    If payment is made automatically online

        Bank _____

        Web site _____

        Phone number _____

        E-mail _____

        Account number _____
        Amount _____
        User name _____
        Password _____

Vehicle Insurance

        Insurance company _____
        Policy number _____
        Web site _____
        Location _____
        Phone number _____
        E-mail _____
        Account number _____
        If payment is made automatically online
                Bank _____
                Web site _____
                Phone number _____
                E-mail _____
                Account number _____
                Amount _____
                User name _____
                Password _____

Additional Vehicles

(Boat, motorcycle, plane, etc.)

        Title _____
        Make and model of vehicle _____
        Color _____
        Location of extra keys _____
        License plate number _____
        Current value _____
        Location of vehicle (garage, slip or hangar number) _____
        Contact person _____
        Phone number _____

If there is a bank note for the vehicle

        Bank _____
        Web site _____
        Location _____
        Phone number _____

E-mail _____

Account number _____

If payment is made automatically online

     Bank _____

     Web site _____

     Phone number _____

     E-mail _____

     Account number _____

     Amount _____

     User name _____

     Password _____

Accounts

List the following information for accounts.

Bank Account(s)

Bank _____

Web site _____

Location _____

Phone number _____

E-mail _____

Account number(s) _____

Type of account _____

Balance _____

User name _____

Password _____

Investment and Brokerage Firms

Investment or brokerage firm _____

Web site _____

Location _____

Phone number _____

E-mail _____

Account number(s) _____

Type of account _____

Current value _____

User name _____

Password _____

Bonds

Name of bond _____

Type of bond _____

Interest rate _____

Current value _____

Date purchased _____

Due date of bond _____

Mutual Funds

Name of fund _____

Amount of shares _____

Current value _____

Date purchased _____

Stocks

Name of stock _____

Amount of shares _____

Current total value _____

Date purchased _____

Preferred stock? _____

Limited Partnerships

Name of partnership _____

Web site _____

Location _____

Phone number _____

E-mail _____

Title _____

Date purchased _____

Current value _____

K-1 Tax Form for Partnership from prior tax year _____

Employee Benefits (if you are entitled to benefits from an employer)

Employer _____

Web site _____

Location _____

Phone number _____

E-mail _____

Type of benefit(s) available (pension, death or dismemberment benefit, etc.) _____

_____

_____

_____

Life Insurance

Insurance company _____

Policy number _____

Web site _____

Location _____

Phone number _____

E-mail _____

Type of policy _____

User name _____

Password _____

If payment is made automatically online

Bank _____

Web site _____

Phone number _____

E-mail _____

Account number _____

Amount _____

User name _____

Password _____

Miscellaneous Holdings

Additional benefits _____

Royalties _____

Copyrights _____

Business holdings _____

Outstanding Amounts Due to You (if you lent money to anyone)

Payer _____

Title _____

Outstanding balance _____

Due date _____

Security for note, if applicable _____

Utilities

Phone

Name of provider _____
Web site _____
Location _____
Phone number _____
E-mail _____
Account number _____
User name _____
Password _____
If payment is made automatically online

Bank _____
Web site _____
Phone number _____
E-mail _____
Account number _____
Amount _____
User name _____
Password _____

Cable and Internet

Name of provider _____
Web site _____
Location _____
Phone number _____
E-mail _____
Account number _____

User name _____
Password _____
If payment is made automatically online

     Bank _____
     Web site _____
     Phone number _____
     E-mail _____
     Account number _____
     Amount _____
     User name _____
     Password _____

Electric Company

Name _____
Web site _____
Location _____
Phone number _____
E-mail _____
Account number _____
User name _____
Password _____
If payment is made automatically online

     Bank _____
     Web site _____
     Phone number _____
     E-mail _____
     Account number _____
     Amount _____
     User name _____
     Password _____

Gas Company

Name _____
Web site _____
Location _____
Phone number _____
E-mail _____
Account number _____

User name _____

Password _____

If payment is made automatically online

      Bank _____

      Web site _____

      Phone number _____

      E-mail _____

      Account number _____

      Amount _____

      User name _____

      Password _____

Garbage collection

Name _____

Web site _____

Location _____

Phone number _____

E-mail _____

Account number _____

User name _____

Password _____

If payment is made automatically online

      Bank _____

      Web site _____

      Phone number _____

      E-mail _____

      Account number _____

      Amount _____

      User name _____

      Password _____

Credit Cards

Account #1

Issuing bank or company _____
Web site _____
Location _____
Phone number _____
E-mail _____
Account number _____
User name _____
Password _____

If payment is made automatically online

      Bank _____
      Web site _____
      Phone number _____
      E-mail _____
      Account number _____
      Amount _____
      User name _____
      Password _____

Account #2

      Issuing bank or company _____

      Web site _____

      Location _____

      Phone number _____

      E-mail _____ _____

      Account number _____

      User name _____

      Password _____

      If payment is made automatically online

           Bank _____

           Web site _____

           Phone number _____

           E-mail _____

           Account number _____

           Amount _____

           User name _____

           Password _____

Account #3

      Issuing bank or company _____

      Web site _____

      Location _____

      Phone number _____

      E-mail _____

      Account number _____

      User name _____

      Password _____

      If payment is made automatically online

           Bank _____

           Web site _____

           Phone number _____

           E-mail _____

           Account number _____

           Amount _____

           User name _____

           Password _____

Account #4

Issuing bank or company _____
Web site _____
Location _____
Phone number _____
E-mail _____
Account number _____
User name _____
Password _____
If payment is made automatically online

    Bank _____
    Web site _____
    Phone number _____
    E-mail _____
    Account number _____
    Amount _____
    User name _____
    Password _____

Online Accounts

E-mail provider

    Account #1

        User name _____

        Password _____

    Account #2

        User name _____

        Password _____

Facebook

    User name _____

    Password _____

Twitter

    User name _____

    Password _____

LinkedIn

    User name _____

    Password _____

Amazon.com

      User name _____

      Password _____

eBay.com

      User name · _____

      Password _____

PayPal.com

      User name _____

      Password _____

Apple iTunes

      User name _____

      Password _____

Personalize the following information for additional accounts.

Account

      User name _____

      Password _____

Account

      User name _____

      Password _____

Account

User name _____
Password _____

Account

User name _____
Password _____

Account

User name _____
Password _____

Account

User name _____
Password _____

Account

User name _____
Password _____

Safe Deposit Boxes and Safes

Safe Deposit Box

Location(s) of safe deposit box
    Bank _____
    Web site _____
    Location _____
    Phone number _____
    E-mail _____
    Account number _____
Location of keys _____
Combination _____

Safe

Location(s) of safe _____
Location of keys _____
Combination _____

Wills, Trusts, Power of Attorney, and Medical Directives

Will

Location of will _____

Lawyer or law firm who drafted and kept will _____

Contact information

    Name _____

    Web site _____

    Location _____

    Phone number _____

    E-mail _____

    Account number _____

Location of keys _____

Combination _____

Trust

Location of trust _____

Lawyer or law firm who drafted and kept trust _____

Contact information

    Name _____

    Web site _____

    Location _____

    Phone number _____

    E-mail _____

    Account number _____

Power of Attorney

    Name _____

    Relation to you or your family _____

    Location _____

    Phone number _____

    E-mail _____

    School or work

        Name _____

        Web site _____

        Location _____

        Phone number _____

        Contact person _____

        E-mail _____

    Location of document _____

    Lawyer or law firm who drafted and kept document

        Name _____

        Bank _____

        Web site _____

        Location _____

        Phone number _____

        E-mail _____

        Account number _____

Medical Directive

    Location of document _____

    Lawyer or law firm who drafted and kept document

    Contact information

        Bank _____

        Web site _____

        Location _____

        Phone number _____

        E-mail _____

        Account number _____

Final Wishes

Care of Your Remains

○ Cremation
○ Burial
○ Donate your body to science

I. Cremation

What to do with your ashes
○ Scattered .
○ Buried
○ Interned
Location
Web site _____
Location _____
Phone number _____
E-mail _____

II. Burial

Where you would like to be buried
Name _____
Web site _____
Location _____
Phone number _____
E-mail _____
Account number _____

If you have purchased a cemetery plot

    Name _____

    Web site _____

    Location _____

    Phone number _____

    E-mail _____

    Account number _____

What sort of headstone you would like

_____

_____

What the headstone should say

_____

_____

If you have purchased a headstone

    Name _____

    Web site _____

    Location _____

    Phone number _____

    E-mail _____

    Account number _____

III. Donate your body to science

    The company you would prefer _____

        Name _____

        Web site _____

        Location _____

        Phone number _____

        E-mail _____

        Account number _____

If the donation is pre-arranged

    Name _____

    Web site _____

    Location _____

    Phone number _____

    E-mail _____

    Account number _____

Funeral or Memorial Service

Indicate whether you prefer a traditional funeral or memorial service, and if you have specific requests or instructions.

At the service

Who should officiate _____

Who should deliver the eulogy _____

Poems to be read _____

_____

_____

Music to be played _____

_____

Type of flowers _____

_____

_____

Who should be pallbearers _____

_____

Charity to donate in your name _____

_____

_____

Additional requests _____

_____

_____

Preference of church, synagogue, or other

    Name _____

    Web site _____

    Location _____

    Phone number _____

    E-mail _____

If the services are pre-paid

    Name _____

    Web site _____

    Location _____

    Phone number _____

    E-mail _____

    Account number _____

How you would like to be memorialized

    Conservancy _____

    Foundation _____

    Donation _____

    Scholarship fund _____

    Adopt an animal _____

Other

    Name _____

    Web site _____

    Location _____

    Phone number _____

    E-mail _____

Dedicate a

    Park bench _____

    Bridge _____

    Garden _____

    Tree _____

    Other _____

Preferred site for memorial

    Name _____

    Web site _____

    Location _____

    Phone number _____

    E-mail _____

If your memorialization is pre-arranged

    Name _____

    Web site _____

    Location _____

    Phone number _____

    E-mail _____

    Account number _____

Special requests or information for your obituary

Distribution of Personal Possessions

Assign valuables and personal possessions to beneficiaries. You may think that everyone can work out who gets what after you're gone, but family feuds have erupted over the smallest items that hold sentimental, personal, or monetary value.

NOTE: Your directives can only be considered legal and binding if you designate them in a valid will. This worksheet, however, can serve as a blueprint for what you can give to your lawyer to put in your will.

Items to designate

- Art
- Jewelry
- Clothing
- Ceramics
- Silverware
- China
- Books
- Furniture
- Rugs
- Collectors items
- Antiques
- Electronics
- Computers and software
- Other

What goes to charity

Name _____

Web site _____

Location _____

Phone number _____

E-mail _____

_____

_____

_____

_____

_____

_____

_____

_____

What goes to your spouse

_____

_____

_____

_____

_____

_____

_____

_____

_____

_____

What goes to your children

_____

_____

_____

_____

_____

_____

_____

_____

_____

_____

_____

What goes to your mother

What goes to your father

What goes to your sibling(s)

What goes to your friends

What goes to other family members

Made in the USA
Monee, IL
26 May 2020

31956174R00046